My name is ...

Gandhi

mantra lingua

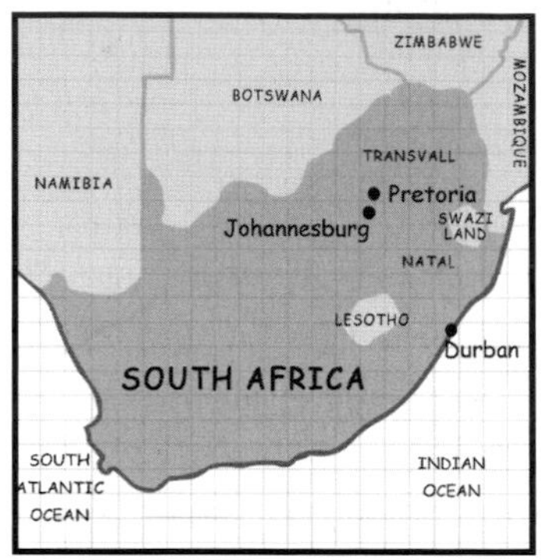

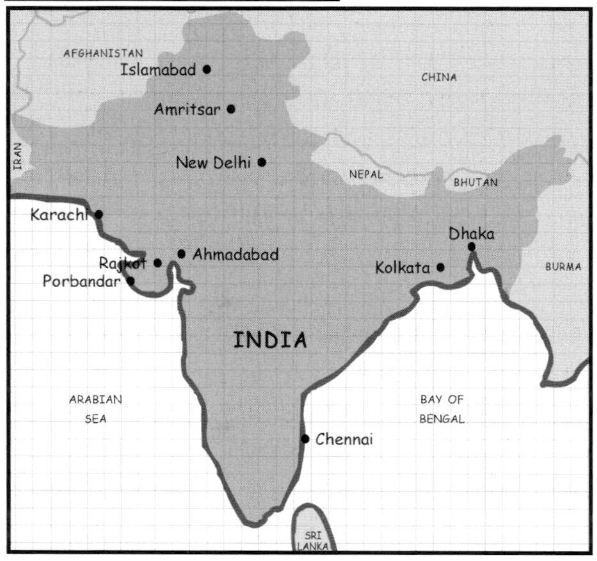

Illustrated by Mariona Cabassa
Spanish text by Lara Toro
English text by Enebor Attard

First published by Parramón Ediciones, S.A. Barcelona, Spain

Mantra Lingua Ltd
Global House
303 Ballards Lane
London N12 8NP UK
www.mantralingua.com

Hello...

You might have seen my picture on TV or read about me in a book. You might even have seen the film they made about my life. I looked very thin and weedy, but don't be fooled. Appearances can be deceptive. During my life I wasn't a sportsman or an inventor. I didn't make lots of money or ride around in fancy cars. Yet when I died millions of people all around the world cried because I was such a great man. I spent my life fighting for those who were born into a life of poverty and hardship just because of the colour of their skin. I fought so that my people would be free. I fought for the independence of my country and, for this, I was called Babu of the Nation - Father of India.

A famous writer once called me Mahatma meaning "Great Soul". He gave me that name because I did so many things for other people and I never once used force or violence. In fact, I proved that violence does nothing towards equality between men and women. War is like a monster that kills people and ruins countries. Words, determination and stubbornness are the best weapons to fight an enemy with. A pen can be more powerful than a gun.

Even though I died in 1948 I still live on in many people's hearts. I am remembered as one of the greatest peacemakers ever.

A Very Devoted Family

My name is Mohandas Karamchand Gandhi. I was born on October 2nd 1869 in Porbandar, a small fishing town by the Arabian Sea in Gujarat, west of India.

At that time India was a British Colony and was not recognised as an independent country. We were part of Britain's empire. However, we felt very strongly about our own sense of self and identity. We had our ancient history and religions, our customs and languages. We wanted to define our own destiny.

My father Karamchand Gandhi was the Prime Minister of Porbandar and was appointed by the King of Gujarat. His job took him away from home much of the time and it was my mother, Putibali, who took care of my brothers and me. My mother and father were quite different from each other but they were both strong people. I admired them in their different ways. My father for being a leader in the community trying to keep control and order; my mother for being a great mum who was always there for us in our growing up years.

When I was seven we moved to Rajkot, a major town in Gujarat. I don't know if you've ever had to move and change schools but I hated it. I wasn't like other children. While my friends liked playing cricket or just hanging out, I liked going for walks on my own. Some people thought I was a bit strange but I wasn't bothered by that. I was happy just being me.

At school I wasn't a good student; my grades weren't that wonderful. But I didn't like it when teachers tried to correct or change my work. I felt like they were trying to tell me what to write.

We were vegetarians, like most Hindus. But I was a bit of a rebel. I tried eating meat when one of my friends told me that the British ruled our country because the meat they ate made them strong. I wanted to be strong so I ate some meat without my parents knowing. I felt really bad lying to them so I quickly gave it up.

An Early Marriage

I was only 13 when I married Kasturbai, my wife of more than 60 years. At that time it was normal in India for families to arrange marriages between children, and some children were married even by the age of six. You would have the wedding but went back to your parents' homes. You only lived together much later.

Our marriage got off to a rocky start. We argued a lot at the beginning because we hardly knew each other and we both had strong personalities. But as I got to know Kasturbai better I grew to love and respect her.

While I was still at school I got in with a bad lot. I smoked and even stole. I started to feel bad about what I'd done and wrote a note to my father asking for forgiveness and to be punished. My father was very ill at the time and confined to bed. I watched him read the note and tears rolled down his face, wetting the paper. He closed his eyes in thought and then tore up the note. It made me cry. I could see my father's agony. I'd thought he would be angry,

but because I had come clean my father forgave me. In fact it made him feel safe about me and brought us closer together.

I was only 16 years old when he died. It was one of the saddest days of my life. I felt that I had failed him. I had wanted to make him proud of me and yet I hadn't achieved anything.

I really wanted to study Medicine, but I was advised that it would be better if I went to England to study Law. I was told that if I became a barrister I could become a Prime Minister like my father and grandfather. My mum would only let me go if I promised to stay faithful to my religion - not to drink wine or eat meat. I gladly agreed. I was 18 years old when I set sail for London in 1888. I had to leave my wife and son in India.

A Truly Spiffing English Gentleman

I had read about England in books and seen lots of pictures of the people and the buildings. I thought of it as a magical land. I wanted to become a true English gentleman so I bought the right clothes: a black suit, white shirts with wing collar, cufflinks and a tie. To finish it off I bought a silk hat costing 19 shillings - about £1.00 which was a lot of money in those days. I went to dance classes and learned the violin. But the hardest bit was learning English.

But I couldn't feel at home in London. It was a cold and damp place and I missed the light and heat of India. I missed my family and most of all I missed home cooking. In those days you could not get garlic, ginger and spices easily. I found one vegetarian restaurant so that I could keep my promise to my mother.

I left London in June 1891 when I passed my final Law exams at Inner Temple. After three intense years in London I could finally return to my homeland.

Religion

In London I read the Bhagavad-Gita (*Song of God*) for the first time. It is one of the holy books for Hindus. In it Lord Krishna explains to his disciple Arjuna, a great warrior, about duty and responsibility to future generations and the courage that must come in living a good life. God has defined what you are, what your children will be and their children. We are mere specks in the scale of outer space and future time. Life is about releasing your fear to go with this 'cosmic' flow. It is things like anger, pride, greed, excuses, false morality that stop us. Who is this "God" you may ask? The Hindu teachers tried to explain who God was, which is very difficult, and that is why there are so many images of God in Hinduism.

I learned about Islam and Christianity. I realized how brave you must be to tell the truth, to live without anger and to forgive those who hurt you. You will need great courage but if you can do this you will be rewarded, not with things, but with a calm nature, free from fear. It amazed me that Jesus was a poor man from a humble family which was so unlike the kings and queens in Hindu stories.

I knew that religion would be my support for the days ahead. Religion has been the foundation of most of man's civilisation and great works on art, music, architecture, literature has been inspired by it. Unfortunately, there has also been horrendous acts of cruelty also done in its name.

Return to India

As soon as I arrived back in India my brother Laxmidas told me mother had died a few weeks before. The woman I loved had died without me even being able to say goodbye. My new life in India had started sadly. Just like when my father died, I had to learn to cope and in a way I became a stronger person.

I decided to teach Kasturbai and my son how to speak English. I knew immediately that this would give them confidence in case I had to go away again or was taken away! And anyway, I wanted them to know the many English customs that I loved at the time.

I also had to earn some money to keep my family. As we no longer had the connections that were needed for me to become a minister I set up my own legal practice. However, when I stood up in court for the first time the most awful thing happened - I was so struck by nerves that words failed me, I couldn't say a single sentence. I felt a complete fool.

You may be surprised to know that I was a total failure as a barrister and in the end I earned money by writing official documents for those who needed them. This was boring but at least it earned money. Then, luckily my knowledge of English got me a job working for a businessman in Durban, South Africa in 1893. He wanted me to represent his company.

Like India, South Africa was also a part of the vast British Empire that ruled over much of the world at the time; it was also a British Colony. This made it easier for Indians to emigrate and start businesses over there.

The

Adversity in Africa

I was 24 when I arrived in South Africa. Little did I realise how my time there was going to change the course of India's history. In South Africa I immediately became acutely aware of colour prejudice. The white skinned Europeans had all the privileges and they looked down on Africans and Asians. Families, education, careers, places you stayed in, even the toilets you could use were based on the colour of your skin.

It was on a train to Pretoria that I first experienced racism. I was travelling first class when a white man got on the train and demanded that the ticket inspector throw me into the third class carriage. Non-whites were not supposed to travel first class. I refused to move. So I was kicked off the train and my luggage taken away. What would you have done? It was winter, bitterly cold. I sat all night shivering on the platform before the next train came. Of course I had to go third class.

Another time I took a stagecoach and had to sit with the coachman on the box outside, while the white conductor sat inside with the white passengers.

When the conductor wanted a smoke he spread a piece of dirty sack-cloth on the footboard and ordered me to sit on it so that he could have my seat outside. I refused. The conductor started beating me up and tried to throw me off but I clung on. Some of the white passengers protested and forced the conductor to let me stay in my seat and finish the journey in peace.

Should I stay and fight for my rights or go back to India? Going back would be like running away and that would make me a coward. It was time to stand up for myself and my people.

First Fights against Injustice

I was so angry that I call a meeting of the Indian community in Pretoria. You may ask why I did not include the African community. I felt that that would be too difficult to organise since even brown and blacks were separated. We needed to be focused and act quickly. I gave my first public speech about all the terrible things that were being done to us. We decided to form an association to look after the other Indian settlers.

The position of the Indians and other non-white people in the Transvaal was dreadful. We had to pay a poll tax of £3; we were not allowed to own land except in a kind of ghetto; we were not allowed to vote. We were not even allowed to walk on the pavement or be out of doors after nine in the evening unless we had special permits. Would you have put up with that?

I went back to India to let everybody know about the terrible way Indians were being treated in South Africa. I travelled all around India giving speeches and handing out the pamphlets I'd written. We needed support, people who were not frightened to march and protest. We needed money. We needed action.

Many people came and this time I took my family with me to South Africa. I'd become a bit of a celebrity in India and amongst my own people, like a popstar or footballer.

The authorities however didn't want me telling everybody how Indians were treated in South Africa and they made their feelings clear. There had been all kinds of rumours that I was bringing a boatload of people to settle in Natal and take away even the land that was marked for the Africans. When our ship arrived there were thousands of people at the dockside. They threatened to drown us all. They then changed their minds and decided to let us off the ship. But when they saw me they started throwing stones and kicking and hitting me. If it hadn't been for a brave English woman they would have killed me. Unfortunately I did not get her name.

The Boer War

In 1899 a brutal and bloody war began in South Africa between the Dutch and the British. It was a war about power, territory, and control. Both groups wanted to own South Africa and when they felt that all diplomatic means had failed they declared war on each other. It was called the Boer War because the descendents of the former Dutch people who had settled down here are called Boers.

If we helped the British in their war, I thought, then they would in turn give us our rights and treat us as equals. And the best way to fight was, not with guns and cannons, but with plasters and stretchers. So I set up the Indian Ambulance Corps in Natal. At the time the British were losing and there were many wounded soldiers. Our job was to take water to the troops in the battlefield and bring back the wounded. We led mules carrying heavy loads of water to the front line. As you can imagine it was very risky, the mules were very slow and we were sitting targets. A large number of us were killed in the cross-fire but unfortunately nobody kept a count of how many died.

When the war ended in 1901 there were many medals and hurrahs, but nothing for the brave Indians.

A Very Unusual Farm

Have you ever heard of the Sermon on the Mount? It's in the Bible, the Christian Holy Book. It's about Jesus climbing to the top of a hill and talking about all those people who, due to the life they led, would find happiness. It says: "Blessed are the poor, for theirs is the kingdom of heaven...
Blessed are the meek, for they shall inherit the earth."

This religious text moved me deeply. Here was a God who talked to the poor and oppressed, the very people who were ignored by the rich and successful. Jesus's life gave me strength. I fought for those who didn't have much and I stood up to bullies. I was convinced that change would happen, if you persevered, even against impossible odds. I prayed, to the God of the Hindus, Muslims and Christians. I prayed that my love for my common men would never leave me, if ever I was successful.

I decided to live on a farm, to shed my ties and lawyers clothes and to feel the life of a common man. We called the farm 'Phoenix' which symbolises rebirth. We led a very simple life. We worked the land, ate simple food, meditated and discussed politics. We did everything ourselves. We washed our own clothes, grew our own vegetables. When someone was ill I treated them with my own cures, based on light meals and natural ointments that the Hindus talked so much of. I learnt how to be a midwife and deliver babies. That's why I was able to be with my wife when she delivered my other two sons.

Ashram Phoenix became very famous. British journalists flocked to write articles about our way of life and my struggle against the Government. We discussed power, colonialism, revolution, politics. Simple living; high thinking! Action was the key to change, thinking on its own was not enough. It was here that we discussed how we could get justice and change. It was here that we found our unique weapon to change the world!

Non-violent Opposition

Just to remind you, the authorities were still treating us as second-class citizens without basic rights and liberties. We had to do something, but how? My Hindu readings taught me about 'Ahimsa' or 'powerful non-violence'. I knew that using violence would be a political mistake. Unjust means could never produce a just outcome. We had to use powerful non-violent ways like speeches, letters, newspaper articles, marches, breaking a bad law and accepting arrest, physical pain, solitary confinement. We had to show people in power and people who 'just did not care' that ours was a cause to take notice.
I knew we had a powerful weapon!

People assumed that if someone hit you, you would hit back. But if you 'turned the other cheek', if you startle them by remaining calm and courageous, would you not surprise them? Would they not think, "Hey, what's this about? Fight, damn you!" I believed strongly that people would respond to the basic good in them and it was fear that made them hostile, angry, violent. I knew how difficult it is to follow non-violence in a violent world. You would require courage and strength to hold onto your beliefs even while you are being physically beaten and abused. Yet we needed a word, a slogan, to help us through the torture that lay ahead, and this word I called "Satyagraha" from the Hindu texts meaning "holding firm to the truth you believe in".

In 1907 the weapon of non-violent opposition was used for the first time. One of the things that the rulers made us do was to always carry our residence permits wherever we went.

This was a paper that allowed us to live in a foreign country. They also made us register our names on official documents so that they would know exactly how many Indians lived in South Africa.

Would you have put up with having to carry these sort of permits all the time? Why should they have the right to discriminate against us? By having to carry permits I felt as if we were being branded and treated like cattle. I decided to defy this unfair law by lighting a fire in public and burning my permit. I encouraged others to do the same.

As you can imagine the authorities didn't like us disobeying their orders. I was arrested and thrown into prison for two months. This was my first time in jail but I wasn't a criminal, I was a political prisoner. I wasn't allowed out of my cell so I spent my time reading and meditating.

A Good Russian Friend

I read many books by many different writers including John Ruskin and Henry David Thoreau. Amongst the books that really impressed me were the works of a Russian writer called Leo Tolstoy. He described the horrors of war in his epic book, *War and Peace*. Just like me he believed that the best way to fight was the peaceful way, without using violence. I related to Pierre, the main character in the book, a big strong man who shunned violence.

Tolstoy once wrote "The man who suffers and offers no resistance helps to free the world." This gave me great strength.

I couldn't travel to Russia to meet this remarkable man. My own people in South Africa needed me. But I wrote to him, explaining to him my ideas about freedom and my unique way of fighting for it. This was the start of a beautiful friendship and we wrote many letters to each other.

As you can imagine our struggle was expanding and more and more people were joining our cause. We had to build a second farm which I was proud to name 'Tolstoy'.

The Magna Carta of the Indians

In 1909 I was arrested again but this time they sentenced me to hard labour. They took me to see General Smuts and I pleaded the case for the Indians. He was sympathetic and made lots of promises, but as I thought, he did not have the power to keep any of them.

One of the next things the Government did was to outlaw all marriages, which were not between Christians. How could the marriages of Muslims and Hindus suddenly not be valid? This was the straw that broke the camels back and now my wife Kasturbai and the other Indian women joined the struggle. The women from the Tolstoy farm managed to persuade the Indian miners to strike. The women were arrested but the strike spread. Thousands of miners and Indian men and women marched in protest behind me to the Transvaal border.

Needless to say I was arrested again, but the campaign of Satyagraha spread. At one point there were 50,000 labourers on strike and several thousands of Indians in jail.

The Government tried repression and even shooting people but in the end we were too strong for them. I was released and in January 1914, a provisional agreement was arrived at between General Smuts and myself. Our main demands had been met. All the agreements were written into the Magna Carta of the Indians in South Africa, signed in the same year.

When I was let out of prison I gave General Smuts my sandals, as a humble token of my gratitude to him. He was rather amused and wore them often.

Some years later I received a parcel and a letter from General Smuts. My sandals were in the parcel. In the letter he explained how much he admired me for everything I had done for my people. He explained how he felt he couldn't fill my shoes because I was such a venerable person, so he asked me to wear the sandals myself. I felt extremely confident. Satyagraha was working!

Return To India...Again

I was excited. Victory in South Africa meant that I wasn't needed here anymore. It was time to fight for the independence of my country. When I arrived in India there were thousands of people shouting and cheering. They had heard what I'd done in South Africa and they treated me like a king.

And there was more. One of the people who welcomed me with a big hug was Rabindranath Tagore. He was a Bengali writer, poet, painter and composer who was famous all over the world. He even won the Nobel Prize for literature, one of the most important prizes in the world. When Tagore saw me he called me Mahatma, which means "Big Soul". I felt completely overwhelmed.

Since that day many people called me Mahatma Gandhi.

The Spinning Wheel

It was true that we had the British Government to thank for building factories, railways and roads, and other technological developments. But as in many countries these improvements only widened the gap between rich and poor people. It was the same during the Industrial Revolution in Britain. People left the countryside to work in overcrowded towns, sometimes in appalling conditions.

In India most people worked in the fields, farming their own food and looking after their animals. There was a self-sufficiency which was like Ashram Phoenix in a way. I thought we should listen to the farmers because I believed they represented the essence of our country ... Simple living; high thinking! I founded the Ashram Satyagraha, the first of many ashrams around India.

I realised that my image, as a leader, would be very important to inspire the people in the days ahead. I was a town's person, used to English customs, a Westerner you may say. I decided to remove my western clothes for the last time and put on a simple white cotton cloth, a dhoti, which most very ordinary people wore. Little did I realise that this gesture, a dhoti, sandals and simple round rimmed spectacles would distinguish me from nearly everyone else in the world. It symbolised me, people just had to look at pictures of me and know what I was about. It was like a flag!

I strongly believed in self-sufficiency. If we can't make something we should not have it. So I started to make my own cotton thread from which dhoti fabric was made. No expensive

machine was used, just a simple spinning wheel made from wood. Everyone could have one and no-one needed to work in the very gloomy and dusty textile factories with their noisy machines.

The spinning wheel too became a symbol for freedom, a statement of how I saw what the new India was about. Simplicity in kind; sophisticated in mind! Many people call this Gandhian economics today.

In Favour Of Untouchables

Hinduism is a religion where everyone is divided into set groups called castes. You were born into a caste and could not move into another by your wishes. The castes were essential for the world to roll forwards into the future. If everyone knew what they had to do in their lives on earth then the world would be safe for future generations. There were basically four castes, each dependent on the other like a football team, with forwards and backs. Up front were the Brahmins, who were the protectors of knowledge and spiritual wisdom. They were the thinkers, the priests, the teachers. Then there were the Kshatriyas (pronounced Kho-tri-ahs) - the warriors, princes and kings who protected the land from invasion and ensured that there was law and order. Next were the group my family belonged to, the Vaisias - the people who provided the commerce, the businessmen who made things to buy. They kept the economy moving. Finally, there were the Sudras, who were the workers, the servants, farmers and craftsmen who were needed just as much as the others to keep the whole society stable.

That was the logic of the Hindu social thinking, oh, about 1000 years before the birth of Jesus Christ!

But as time moved on, the population increased, new people came and others went, and many people did not fit into this easy grouping. There were Indians who did not fit into any caste. They are called the 'pariahs' or outcastes, and gradually, because they did not belong, the rest of the people called them 'untouchables'. They were exploited, poor, and the victims of prejudice. Nobody wanted to come near them, they could not drink water from the same tap as the upper-castes, they could not vote, they could not pray in the same temples, they had no rights. They lived in squalor. The men and women could do no better than cleaning toilets and clearing rubbish off the streets. The problem was that you were seen as a pariah just because you were born into a family with no caste. They called themselves 'Dalits', literally meaning 'broken people'.

I spent some time travelling around the country. I wanted to get to know India and her people better. I saw for myself the cruel way that the untouchables were treated. It was wrong! How could we accuse the British Government of crimes when we allowed such things to go on? I decided to fight for the rights of the untouchables and give them back their dignity.

It would be difficult. Fighting an outside enemy is easy compared to changing long-established habits within the family. I renamed the untouchables and called them 'Harijans' meaning 'children of God'. I insisted on restoring some of their rights and invited them to live in my ashram in Ahmedabad. I was not fighting to abolish the caste system, for it was an important part of our ancient Hindu tradition. But what I really wanted to do was to stop people treating the untouchables badly. They would have a greater say in whatever decisions that might affect our country. I wanted to end the segregation.

Later, long after my death, the President of India was a Harijan!

A Strike To Remember

In 1914 a great war broke out in Europe. I campaigned in India for people to go and fight on the side of the British. 130,000 Indian soldiers were fighting in France by 1915, in what became known as the First World War. When it ended in 1918 we again hoped that our contribution would be rewarded.

But our fingers were burnt for a second time. Just like after the Boer War, far from being grateful, the British Government decided to deny our right to independence all the more. We felt betrayed and cheated. I decided that it was time to use the weapon of Satyagraha again.

In 1919 I became the leader of the newly-formed Indian National Congress party and on April 6th I called for a general strike. That day masses of people did not go to work. Many fasted in protest against the British Government's decision not to give us our independence. But not everyone understood the peaceful methods of Satyagraha. Remember, you had to be strong to be non-violent.

Very quickly events turned violent. A number of officials were murdered, and banks, Government offices, and private properties were burnt. Things got worse and worse and in the end I had to call the strike off, to stop the violence. After that, the Government ruled that any public meeting was illegal. What had we gained? Nothing!

Once again I appealed to the people not to obey this crazy law and the strongest popular support came from the Punjabi peoples. On April 13th 1919 thousands of unarmed Punjabi men, women and children gathered in a city called Amritsar, at the Jallianwallah Bagh (Garden) to protest.

The crowd was gathered in a narrow square, from which it was very difficult to leave. Some 50 soldiers and two tanks were sent to surround the square. What happened next was unbelievable! An officer called General Dyer appeared at the front of the group of soldiers. Without a word of warning, he ordered his men to fire into the crowd for about ten minutes. When the people fled from the centre, the bullets followed them. The soldiers fired without pity at the trapped targets. They only stopped when the bullets ran out. There were bodies and blood everywhere! Nearly 400 people were killed!

The Salt March

After the massacre we wanted nothing more to do with the British Government: we refused to buy their goods, our children wouldn't go to their schools, and we would no longer work for them. We blocked streets just by sitting on the ground. The police would beat us but we refused to get up. I always said not to use violence. But once again people were not strong. Some fought with guns and I was arrested again in 1921, though it was nothing to do with me. I was let out in 1924 and thought I would stay out of politics. But that didn't last for long.

I wanted to get rid of unfair laws, like the salt tax. The British Government would take *our* salt from *our* coasts but if we wanted to buy salt we had to pay tax. It was daylight robbery.

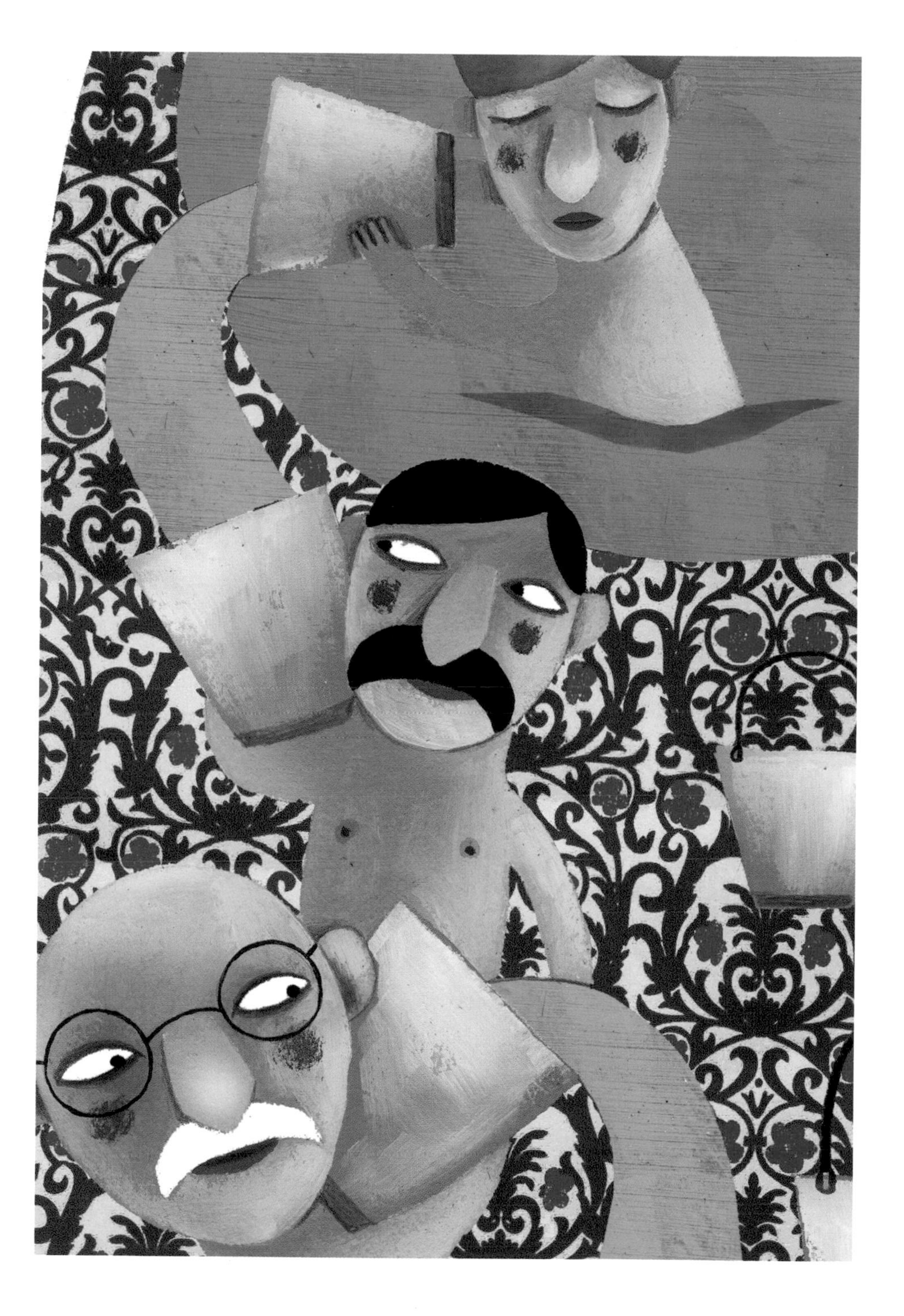

On March 12th 1930 I marched with 78 followers from Ahmedabad towards the sea. We passed through lots of towns and villages where we spoke about the salt tax. Many joined the march. We walked for very nearly a month before we reached the coast. We went into the sea, drew the water and collected the salt. By this simple act we were breaking the law. But also from that moment we no longer paid the tax for our salt.

At the same time my second son drew together a horde of people outside the Government salt factory to prevent any salt being sent out. The authority's response was swift and violent. But we stayed put, choosing to voice our grief through more diplomatic means. This time Satyagraha worked and from that day more and more British people, particularly in the Labour and Liberal parties, started to discuss Independence.

A Meeting in London

In September 1931 I was invited to the second Round Table Conference in London organised by the British to discuss Indian Independence. (I was in prison at the time of the first conference.)

In London, I refused to stay in a hotel. I stayed at Kingsley Hall, a social service centre in the East End, where I met many 'ordinary' working people. I also met many famous people including the distinguished King and Queen who invited me for tea at their palace. Can you imagine me in my dhoti with the King dressed in his beautiful suit with medals! It was quite funny. Then I met the Charlie Chaplin, the famous comic in the movies who had also a huge love for the common people.

During my three months in Britain I visited many poor homes and met many children. I travelled to the Lancashire textile mill towns where factory workers had lost their jobs since we no longer bought their cloth in India. I was surprised to find that even then many of them supported our cause.

The talks in London were not very successful. The British politicians wanted only to give in half way. It is not easy to give up a jewel in the crown! I was not interested in half measures and wanted full independence. We walked out of the talks.

To Fight or not to Fight for Britain

In 1939 war broke out in Europe a second time. The British were fighting the Germans, again. There had always been Indian soldiers and officers in the British Armed Forces just as there had been Indians working in the Civil Service courts, police, tax administration, railways, etc. The Indian soldiers were fighting the Germans in Europe and the Japanese in Burma. The most famous of these were the Gurkhas, but there were many soldiers from the Punjab, Maharastra and Bengal. These were people who did not want to get involved in politics and we knew they would be vital to keep India functioning after independence.

We, the civilians, in India were not really interested in what was going on in the war in Europe. It was too far away. But in December 1941 Japan bombed Pearl Harbour and a year later they had advanced to Burma. Soon they would reach India and suddenly for us the war became real. The British wanted political support for their fight against the Japanese. They offered us devolution which would allow us to govern our own country within the overall control of London. We however wanted total independence, devolution was not enough.

Opinion was fiercely divided amongst the civilians. Some people thought that we should help the British. Others felt that we should let the Japanese take India and then work out our independence. Which was the lesser evil. I was not sure but I had to decide. Remember, politics is about recognising the right moment, being clear of what you want and acting swiftly. In 1942, when the war was not going well for Britain and their Allies, I stood up at the All India Congress Committee and launched the slogan that spread like fire: "Quit India!"

The British Government's response was immediate. Members of the Indian Congress and I were imprisoned. I wrote a letter to the Viceroy of India informing him of our displeasure at being imprisoned unfairly. I began to fast as a protest. I ate nothing for almost three weeks and became very very ill. The Government worried that I might not live. If I died I would become a martyr, causing even more trouble. They let me out of prison but I was so weak that for some time I couldn't even speak.

It was during this time in prison when my beloved wife died. She was old, like me, and we had spent many years together. She was an extraordinary woman who had always supported me. She was my pillar of strength and I missed her.

A Nation Divided

India was a country divided into two major religious groups, Hindus and Muslims. Although we were of the same race, we had different beliefs, different places of worship and different ways of living our lives.

Some people say the British encouraged Muslims to demand more and more for themselves and separate themselves from the Hindus. They called this policy 'divide and rule'. Britain could then be seen as being the only ones who could keep peace in India. By the end of the war in 1945 Britain had been devastated and negotiations for our independence began again. The Muslim League and Mohammad Ali Jinnah, their leader, represented the Muslim people. He wanted a separate country for Muslims which was independent of India and would be called Pakistan.

The British however would only grant us independence if Hindus and Muslims negotiated together. How could you work as a team if at the same time you acted in your own self-interest? Getting independence had become even more difficult.

Then in 1947 everything changed. The new Viceroy, Lord Mountbatten, persuaded Congress to accept Jinnah's demands for the partition of India as a condition for independence. I was against this. Hindus and Muslims had lived together for hundreds of years and they could continue to do so. Breaking India up would be a victory for non-secularism and a huge waste of resources. I pleaded, but time was running out. A deadline was set, a decision had to be made and on August 15th 1947, India and Pakistan were independent of Britain.

I didn't join in the celebrations. The birth of the new nations led to a huge transfer of populations. Muslims didn't feel safe in India and travelled to Pakistan leaving homes and belongings.

Hindus travelled to India, leaving homes and belongings. Chaos and violence was everywhere. How could I celebrate when thousands of people were killing and maiming each other in the name of religion? In the Punjab, families and friends were separated in fearsome killings. In Kolkata and Dhaka, property was looted, revenge killings raged and the future was already looking awful. I felt angry, helpless, hopeless ... my whole life's work being demolished in a few days. I decided to fast, in protest against my own people. Maybe this symbol of despair would bring some sense. I became weaker and weaker and word spread that unless the riots stopped the people's Bapuji would die. On September 4th, the leaders of all communities in Kolkata brought a signed pledge that there would be no more violence and I must live for the sake of their conscience. I broke my fast and the people of Kolkata kept their promise even though in many cities Hindus and Muslims were slaughtering each other. I moved around, helping where I could to drive some sense and fasting when I could not get any. But the body was getting frailer by the minute.

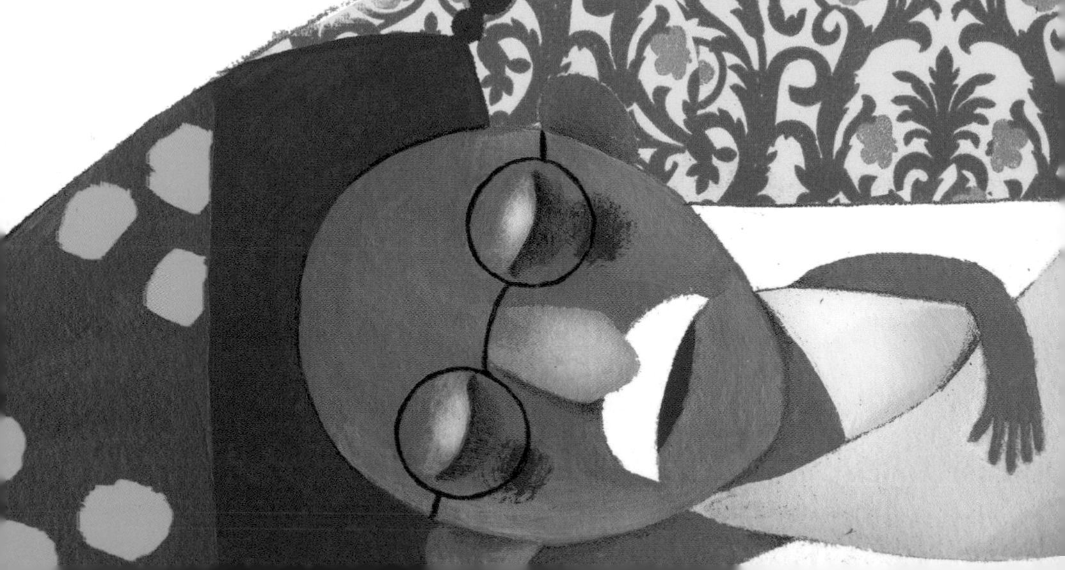

INDIA
PAKISTAN

Goodbye to a Troubled World

During my life I made many friends but also many enemies. Some Hindus saw me as a traitor because I cared for Muslims and helped them during these terrible times. They could not understand how I, a Hindu, could help Muslims and have Muslim friends. They had never really understood what I had preached. Some people wanted to kill me. These fanatics wanted India empty of Muslims even though there were more Muslims living in India than in Pakistan! On January 20th 1948 a bomb went off while I was at evening prayer. Luckily it didn't kill me.

Then came January 30th 1948. A day that started like any other day. It happened in the Gardens of Birla House in New Delhi. I stood on the steps with my two granddaughters and greeted the crowd by putting my hands together. Many people came forward and greeted

me in return. One young man called Nathuram Godse stepped in and before anybody could stop him he pulled out a gun and shot me three times, straight at my heart.

My old body was no match for bullets. As I crumpled to the ground my two granddaughters caught me and watched helplessly as I breathed my last breath.

My values were based on there being respect and dignity between all men and women. I believed that we should always extend a helping hand to our fellow citizens, whether they were Muslims or Hindus, Catholics or Protestants or Jews, black or white. We should live side by side in unity, each person respecting the personal space of another in a world free from fear.

I know my life has been an example for many people. I have given hope, inspiration and belief to millions around the world. I am convinced my actions created more love than hate. Thousands and thousands of people cried at my funeral.

Today, there is a statue of me in every city in India: my thin, dhoti-clad body, the head with very short hair, and a pair of metal framed round glasses resting on my nose. In New Delhi, the capital city, a beacon shines continually in my memory. There is even a statue in Tavistock Square in London. People read about my writings on Satyagraha, and understand why non-violence and love leads to a brilliant state of fearlessness.

The day I died has come to be known as World Peace Day. On that day thousands of people reflect upon peace and pray for a world with no wars, where people of all races and backgrounds will live together as one.

In many schools the walls are covered with banners bearing messages of good wishes and resolutions and painted with great white doves. These birds have become the symbol of peace. Their colour, white, is the same colour as the flags that soldiers wave when they ask for a truce to their enemies. And at the same time it is a living being that can fly, which represents freedom.

That is why if a dove ever flies over your head, don't just let it pass. Instead try to listen to her message, because it will be a message of peace.

I inspired other people to fight for justice and freedom without using violence. People such as Martin Luther King Jnr. in America, Nelson Mandela in South Africa and Daw Aung San Suu Kyi in Burma.

And I am sure many others will follow.

Year	Life of Gandhi	History
1869-1879	1869. Born in Porbandar, Gujarat, India.	The imperialistic colonies spread, especially in the African continent. Third French Republic of Paris.
1880-1890	1882. Married Kasturbai 1885. Death of father 1888. Gandhi goes to London where he studies Law and his mother dies.	The National Indian Congress is founded. Alexander II, the Russian Czar is killed.
1891-1900	1891. Gandhi goes back to India. 1893. He moves to South Africa. 1896. He returns to India to let people know about the trouble in South Africa.	Boer War in South Africa. Beginning of the independence of Cuba. First Olympic Games of the modern era in Athens.
1901-1910	1904. Farm Phoenix is established in South Africa and he founds the Indian Opinion. 1907. He uses Satyagraha or weapon of powerful non-violence for the first time. 1909. Gandhi visits London looking for support. 1910. Farm Tolstoy is founded.	The Muslim League is established. Queen Victoria dies in the United Kingdom. Roald Amundsen reaches the North Pole. The Russian revolution breaks out.
1911-1920	1913. He makes a deal with General Smuts: the Magna Carta of the Indians in South Africa. 1915. He returns to India and he is welcomed as Mahatma. 1915: the farm Satyagraha is founded in Ahmedabad.	The First World War breaks out. A general strike takes place in India and it ends with a massacre in Amritsar. The Treaty of Versailles is signed. The Titanic sinks. Amundsen reaches the South Pole.
1921-1930	He starts the Salt March.	Financial crack of 1929 and economic crisis all over the world. Primo de Rivera's coup d'etat in Spain.
1931-1940	He travels to London to participate in the Second Round Table. 1933. He publishes the magazine Harijan, in favour of the untouchables.	Second World War breaks out and so does the Spanish Civil War. The Commonwealth is established: a community consisting of nations colonised by the British.
1941-1950	1942. Gandhi's wife dies. 1948. Gandhi dies.	Japan invades Burma. Independence of India, creation of Pakistan. United Nations and NATO are created The estate of Israel is created.

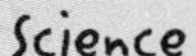

	Arts
1869-1879: the first typing machine is invented. Graham Bell invents the telephone. Edison invents the telegraph and the bulb.	First exhibition of "Impressionism" masterpieces of Art. Tolstoy finishes "War And Peace".
The first automobile with a petrol engine is built. Koch discovers the tuberculosis virus. J J Thomson discovers the "electron".	Eiffel builds the Tower in Paris. Vincent van Gogh paints the picture "Sunflowers".
Röntgen invents X-ray. Freud develops the theory of psychoanalysis.	The Lumière brothers carry out the first cinema show.
Marconi invents the radio. The Wright brothers fly for the first time. Einstein announces the Theory pf Relativity.. Ramón y Cajal wins the Nobel Prize for Medicine.	Pablo Picasso paints "The Ladies of Avignon". Wassily Kandinsky painted his first abstract painting.
The first project of a space shuttle takes place. Niels Bohr suggests the model of hydrogen atom and starts the theory of Quantum Mechanics. Einstein receives Nobel Prize for Physics.	Griffith directs the film "The Birth of a Nation". Kafka writes "The Trial" and "The Metamorphosis".
Fleming discovers penicillin. The human blood types are discovered.	James Joyce writes "Ulysses". The Empire State Building is started. "Micky Mouse" patented.
Chadwick discovers the neutron. The radar is used for the first time. The electronic microscope is invented.	Walt Disney makes "Snow White and the Seven Dwarfs". Pablo Picasso paints "Guernika". The first Superman comic is published
The USA creates the atomic bomb. Waksmann invents streptomycin. The plane, Bell XI, breaks the sound barrier for the first time.	Orson Wells directs "Citizen Kane". George Orwell writes "Animal Farm".

My name is ...

is a collection of biographies of world famous people. In each volume, a historical figure from science, history, art, culture or literature tells us all about their life, their work and the world they lived in. The vivid illustrations allow us to submerge ourselves into their world.

Gandhi

If you would like to find out more about me you can do the following:

1. Visit your local library and look in the reference section where you will find books about me and India.
2. Look in an encyclopedia under my name.
3. Look on the internet where there are many websites including the following ones:

www.web.mahatma.org.in/pictures.jsp
www.channel4.com/learning/main/netnotes/programmeid1339.htm
www.mkgandhi.org
www.atributetohinduism.com